101 Facts About Our World

101 FACTS ABOUT
MOUNTAINS

Julia Barnes

Gareth Stevens Publishing
A WORLD ALMANAC EDUCATION GROUP COMPANY

Please visit our web site at: www.garethstevens.com
For a free color catalog describing Gareth Stevens Publishing's
list of high-quality books and multimedia programs,
call 1-800-542-2595 (USA) or 1-800-387-3178 (Canada).
Gareth Stevens Publishing's fax: (414) 332-3567.

Library of Congress Cataloging-in-Publication Data

Barnes, Julia, 1955-
    101 facts about mountains / by Julia Barnes. — North American ed.
      p. cm. — (101 facts about our world)
    Summary: Describes the characteristics, formation, and erosion of the world's mountains,
  the plants and animals living there, and how to protect their environment.
      Includes bibliographical references and index.
      ISBN 0-8368-3708-8 (lib. bdg.)
      1. Mountain ecology—Juvenile literature.   2. Mountains—Juvenile literature.   [1. Mountains.
  2. Mountain ecology.   3. Ecology.]   I. Title: One hundred one facts about mountains.
  II. Title: One hundred and one facts about mountains.   III. Title: Mountains.   IV. Title.
  QH541.5.M65B37   2003
  551.43'2—dc21   2003045712

This North American edition first published in 2004 by
Gareth Stevens Publishing
A World Almanac Education Group Company
330 West Olive Street, Suite 100
Milwaukee, WI 53212 USA

This U.S. edition copyright © 2004 by Gareth Stevens, Inc. Original edition © 2003 by First
Stone Publishing. First published by First Stone Publishing, 4/5 The Marina, Harbour
Road, Lydney, Gloucestershire, GL15 5ET, United Kingdom. Additional end matter © 2004
by Gareth Stevens, Inc.

First Stone Series Editor: Claire Horton-Bussey
First Stone Designer: Rob Benson
Geographical consultant: Miles Ellison
Gareth Stevens Editors: Catherine Gardner and JoAnn Early Macken

Photographs © Oxford Scientific Films Ltd

Printed in Hong Kong through Printworks Int. Ltd

1 2 3 4 5 6 7 8 9 07 06 05 04 03

You might think that nothing could move a mountain, but mountains are changing all the time. The forces of wind and rain wear away at the rock face, changing its size and shape. Mud, rocks, snow, or ice can slide down a mountainside and destroy everything in the way. A **volcano** can erupt and start a new mountain.

Despite all the hazards, many different kinds of animal and plant life have made homes on mountain slopes. Some enjoy an easy time in the gentle foothills. Others cling to life in the freezing cold conditions at the mountain's peak.

Now, the magnificent mountain scenery and wildlife are threatened as humans claim more and more land. We must try to protect the spectacular beauty of mountains before it is too late.

MAJOR MOUNTAINS OF THE WORLD

Rocky Mountains

Brooks Range

Alaska Range

North Pacific Ocean

Coast Mountains

Mount St. Helens

Cascade Range

Sierra Nevada

Sierra Madre Occidental

Sierra Madre Del Sur

Sierra Madre

NORTH AMERICA

Appalachian Mountains

North Atlantic Ocean

Blue Ridge Mountains

South Pacific Ocean

Andes Mountains

SOUTH AMERICA

South Atlantic Ocean

East Brazilian Highlands

Key

RUSSIAN RANGES:
1. Byrranga Mountains
2. Vablonovyy Range
3. Stanovoy Range
4. Great Khingan Shan (China)
5. Sikhote-Alin Range
6. Dzhugdzhur Range
7. Verkhoyansk Range
8. Cherskogo Range
9. Kolyma Range
10. Koryak Range

⚠ Everest   ⚠ K2

⋮ Main centers of volcanic activity

Division between North and South America

Division between Asia and Africa

Division between Europe and Asia

Division between Asia and Oceania

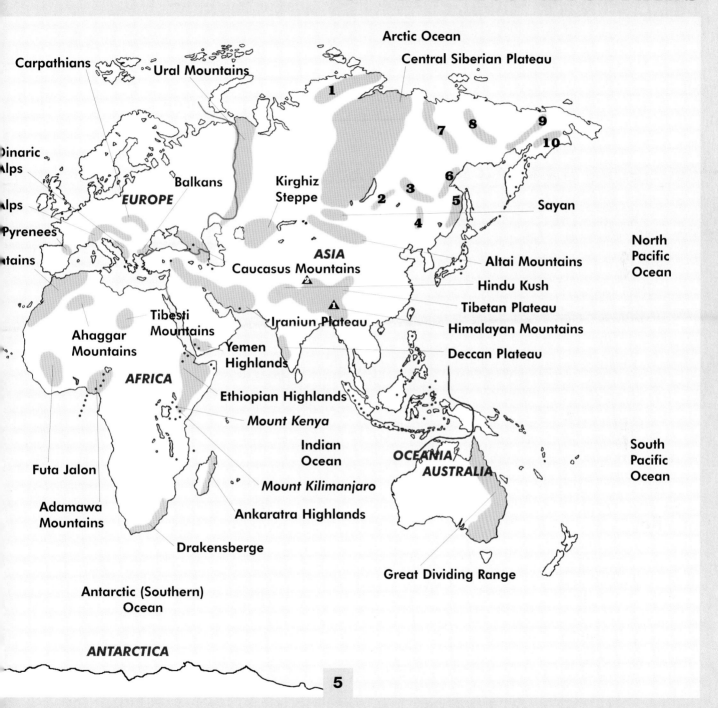

Carpathians

Ural Mountains

Arctic Ocean

Central Siberian Plateau

1

7   8   9

10

Dinaric Alps

Balkans

Kirghiz Steppe

6

Alps

EUROPE

2   3

5

Pyrenees

Caucasus Mountains

ASIA

4

Sayan

tains

North Pacific Ocean

Altai Mountains

Tibesti Mountains

Hindu Kush

Ahaggar Mountains

AFRICA

Iraniun Plateau

Tibetan Plateau

Yemen Highlands

Himalayan Mountains

Ethiopian Highlands

Deccan Plateau

Mount Kenya

Futa Jalon

Indian Ocean

OCEANIA

South Pacific Ocean

Adamawa Mountains

Mount Kilimanjaro

AUSTRALIA

Ankaratra Highlands

Drakensberge

Great Dividing Range

Antarctic (Southern) Ocean

ANTARCTICA

2 A mountain may stand alone, or it may be part of a long chain of mountains that stretches over thousands of miles.

3 Permanent snow may cover a mountaintop (left). Temperatures at the peak can be so cold that few animals or plants can survive.

1 Mountains provide some of the most spectacular scenery in the world and offer homes for many kinds of living things.

4 On the lower slopes, where it is warmer, many different kinds of wildlife make their homes.

5 Mountains change over time. New mountains are being created, and old mountains are being worn away by wind and water.

6 Changes to mountains usually take place very slowly, over millions of years. On the other hand, some changes, such as an eruption of a volcano (right) happen suddenly and violently.

7 Mountains began to take shape five hundred million years ago when the surface of Earth was still forming.

8 A thin layer of rock, called the crust, covers the land and the ocean bed.

9 Powerful forces deep under Earth's surface caused the crust to break in places and form **plates**, or giant pieces.

7

10 Earth's plates are like giant pieces of a jigsaw puzzle. They float around slowly on red-hot liquid rock that lies below the crust layer.

11 At their edges, or **margins**, plates are pushed together.

12 Mountains form along the margins of Earth's plates.

13 The plates bump against each other with so much pressure that the land at the margins is squeezed together.

14 As the plates keep pushing, the land at the margins can only move upward. It forms huge folds in Earth's surface.

15 The mountains that are formed this way are **fold mountains**. They are the biggest and most dramatic of all mountains.

16 Some well-known fold mountain ranges are the Rockies and Appalachians in North America, the Alps (left) in Europe, the Himalayas (right) that cross Nepal and Tibet in southern Asia, and the Andes in South America.

17 The longest range of fold mountains is the Andes, which stretches along the coast nearly 4,500 miles (7,250 kilometers).

18 Some of the longest mountain ranges are under the oceans.

19 The highest peak on the planet is Mount Everest (above), which rises 29,035 feet (8,850 meters) above sea level. Part of the Himalayas, Mount Everest is located in southern Asia.

20 Long ago, the Himalayas were covered by water. Scientists have found the **fossils** of sea creatures in the rocks of the Himalayas.

21 Each of Earth's plates has cracks, called faults, that divide the crust into huge blocks.

22 Blocks of Earth's crust can shift along faults. When the blocks shift up and down, they create **fault block mountains**.

23 Fault block mountains, such as the Sierra Nevada in

California, in the United States, are usually smaller than fold mountains.

24 Fault block and fold mountains are formed by slow movements of Earth's crust, so they take thousands of years to grow.

25 A volcano is a kind of a mountain that can form quickly, sometimes in days, through the buildup of ash and rock.

26 A volcano starts when red-hot liquid rock from deep inside Earth forces its way to the surface and pours out in fiery streams (below).

27 When a volcano erupts (below), **lava,** ash, and rocks build up to form a mountain.

28 An active volcano, or one that erupts regularly, grows taller each time it erupts. Stromboli, in the Lipari Islands near Italy, is an active volcano.

29 A volcano that has not erupted for a long time, such as Mount Fuji in Japan, is dormant. A dormant volcano can suddenly erupt again.

30 Mount Kilimanjaro in Africa is called an extinct volcano. It has completed its active life and will not erupt again.

31 Mountains made by volcanoes change the landscape dramatically and quickly. Other kinds of mountains grow or shrink much more slowly.

32 The Himalayas are about forty million years old. Many mountains wear down over time, but the giant Himalayas keep growing.

33 A young mountain range, such as the Alps in south-central Europe, has rough, jagged peaks.

34 As time goes by, wind and water can wear away the rocks, which makes them smoother and more rounded. This process is called erosion.

35 The Appalachian Mountains (above) in North America are more than 250 million years old. Their smooth, rounded tops are signs of their old age.

36 Erosion works in many ways to alter the shape of a mountain.

37 Millions of years ago during the **Ice Age**, slabs of ice covered parts of Earth. Gigantic **glaciers**, which are like rivers of ice, slowly slipped down the sides of mountains.

38 Glaciers crushed and carved the surfaces of some mountains, changing their shapes.

39 When a river flows down a mountain, it cuts into the rock and creates deep-sided **valleys** (left) and steep **gorges**.

40 Grains of sand and dust carried by the wind and water slowly rub off bits of rock. Acid in rain also helps break apart rocks.

41 Where the rocks on a mountainside have cracked, plants fight to grow (right). They sink their roots into the cracks, looking for water and a foothold on the mountain's surface.

42 Plant roots make the cracks in the rocks wider, and the rocks are forced farther apart.

43 **Lichens** growing on the rocks help break them down.

44 A landslide (below) can occur after a heavy rain. In a landslide, rain loosens mud and rocks, allowing them to crash down the mountainside.

45 As snow melts or falls, it can send snow, ice, and dirt tumbling down the mountain in an avalanche (right).

46 Avalanches and landslides happen suddenly and without any warning. They can destroy everything in their paths.

47 The world's biggest single avalanche took place in 1962 in Peru, South America. It destroyed eight villages and killed 3,500 people in minutes.

48 In the United States, most avalanches are in the Rockies. Avalanches also happen often in Canada, Europe, Peru, and China.

49 Traveling in mountains or climbing up them can be dangerous.

50 Mountain weather can change suddenly. It can be very warm or cold, and the wind can whip up huge storms.

53 Otzi wore leather boots, a jacket, and fur leggings. He carried an axe.

54 Today, some people climb tall mountains for fun. They use ropes and special tools (above) to inch their way up steep cliffs.

51 Ice preserved the body of a man who died five thousand years ago in the Italian Alps.

52 The body of Otzi the Iceman can tell us something about how ancient people tried to live in dangerous climates.

55 Mountain climbing can be dangerous. Climbers must learn safety rules and use helmets and other safety gear.

56 Weather is not the only danger on a mountain. Higher up, the air becomes thinner. It becomes harder and harder for people to breathe and to get enough **oxygen**.

57 Despite the dangers, mountain climbers (right) have tried again and again to tackle the world's highest peaks.

58 In 1786, two mountain climbers reached the top of Mont Blanc, the highest mountain in the Alps.

59 Many people have tried to climb to the top of the mighty Mount Everest. All of these attempts ended in failure until 1953.

61 Hillary and Norgay were on the **summit** for only fifteen minutes. Worried about the lack of oxygen, they took some photographs and climbed right back down.

62 Weather conditions change around the sides of a mountain. The side facing into the wind usually gets the most rain.

60 On May 29, 1953, Edmund Hillary, a climber from New Zealand, and Tenzing Norgay, a **Sherpa** from Nepal, reached the top of Everest.

63 The conditions at the bottom of a tall mountain in a **tropical** area are different than the conditions at the top.

64 In the tropics, the temperature drops 1.4° Fahrenheit (0.7° Celsius) for every 500 feet (152 m) higher. Temperature affects the kinds of animals and plants that can survive.

65 At the bottom of a mountain is an area of flat land, called the plains (left). Conditions on the plains match the surrounding area, with the same animals and plants as in any other rain forest, desert, or dry grassland.

66 A mountainside starts with an area called the foothills. The foothills are slightly cooler than the plains.

67 Trees and flowers grow on mountain slopes (below). In Europe and much of North America, the trees on the slopes are deciduous, which means they lose their leaves in winter.

68 Evergreens, trees that keep their leaves all year, grow in the foothills in tropical regions. They form a rain forest.

69 In Africa, mountain gorillas (left) live among the trees of the foothills. The gorillas live in the tree branches and eat fruit and leaves.

70 Mountain gorillas live in small family groups. A group includes females and their babies led by one large, strong male.

71 Higher up, foothills turn into the **middle slopes**. Conifer trees, such as pines, spruces, and firs, which do not shed their leaves, thrive at this level.

72 Porcupines (below) live in middle-slope forests, feeding on twigs and bark in the winter and plants in the summer.

73 Porcupines have coats of barbed quills. The quills help protect them from other animals.

74 In tropical areas, middle slopes may have bamboo forests, home to red pandas. (See page 3.)

75 Bamboo forests in southwestern China are home to giant pandas (above). Their favorite food is bamboo.

76 People are ruining the bamboo forests. Fewer than one thousand giant pandas live in the wild.

77 Even higher up the mountain is the tree line. Above the tree line, the weather is too cold for trees to grow.

78 Near the tree line, trees struggle to grow. Most look more like bushes than trees.

79 Mountain sheep and goats (below) graze on the steep upper slopes. These animals have thick fur coats to protect them from the cold mountain air.

80 Mountain goats are agile. They have hooves like pincers, so they

can keep their grip on rocky slopes. They must be alert for big mountain cats, which hunt at night.

81 North American mountain lions (right), also known as pumas or cougars, make their homes on rocks high up on the mountainside. Pumas hunt deer and rabbits.

82 Snow leopards live and hunt on the mountains of the Himalayas. They spend summers high on the mountains but live lower in cold weather.

83 Snow leopards have thick pads of fur underneath their feet, so they can walk on the slippery ice and snow.

84 Today, only a few hundred snow leopards are left in the wild.

85 The world's only mountain parrot, the kea (below), makes its nest under rocks.

86 Unlike other parrots, which eat fruit, the kea eats insects and meat. It sometimes attacks sheep with its sharp beak.

87 High up the slope of a mountain is the snow line. Above the snow line, the temperature stays below the freezing point, which is the temperature at which all water stays frozen as ice and snow.

88 The snow line is higher in the warm summer months than it is in the cold winter.

89 Between the tree line and the snow line, plants usually are small, have dark leaves, and grow close to the ground.

26

mountains. They can soar up higher or swoop down lower to find food.

92 The highest spot in the world is home to the Alpine chough (left), a bird related to crows. These birds live among the high tops of the Himalayas.

90 At the summit of a mountain, the dry, cold, windy weather, the ice and snow cover, and the thin, rocky soil make it hard for any kind of plant or animal to survive.

91 Birds have an advantage on

93 Lammergeiers are huge birds from parts of Europe, Africa, and Asia. To feed, they pick up bones of dead animals, fly up high, drop the bones to the ground to smash them, and then eat the **marrow**.

94 Mountains play an important part in the system of collecting and delivering water to the lower places on Earth.

95 Mountains provide special homes for many kinds of animals and plants. As humans take up more space on mountains, however, wildlife suffers.

96 When people carve into mountainsides to mine minerals, such as silver and copper, they can damage animals' homes.

97 In the mountain foothills, trees are cut down to make room for houses. Crops to provide food are being grown farther and farther up the mountain.

98 So many climbers, skiers, bikers, and hikers use mountains that nature suffers. More visitors mean more cars, more roads, and more hotels.

99 As humans move in, animals must move up the mountain to find food and shelter.

100 Animals that need to live on mountains, like mountain gorillas, giant pandas, and snow leopards (below) could die out in the wild.

101 If we do not take good care of our mountains, we will lose these important natural **resources**.

Glossary

fault block mountains: mountains that are formed between fault lines of Earth's crust.

fold mountains: mountains that form when Earth's plates push into each other.

fossils: the remains of animals or plants left in rocks.

glaciers: huge sheets of ice that form in areas where snow falls but never melts.

gorges: narrow valleys with steep sides that were cut by a river.

Ice Age: a time when most of the Earth was covered by glaciers.

lava: red-hot liquid rock.

lichens: algae and fungi that grow together.

margins: the edges of the plates of Earth's crust.

marrow: a soft material in bones used to make blood cells.

middle slopes: the area of a mountain above the foothills and below the tree line.

oxygen: a gas in the air that we need to breathe.

plates: giant pieces of Earth's crust.

resources: things that have value.

Sherpa: a member of an ethnic group in Nepal that guides mountain climbers.

summit: the top of a mountain.

tropical: having high temperatures and heavy rainfall.

valleys: channels cut through hills by a river.

volcano: a violent eruption of hot liquid rock from beneath Earth's surface.

More Books to Read

**Fragile Mountains
(Environment Alert series)**
Paula Z. Hogan
(Gareth Stevens)

**How Mountains are Made
(Let's Read and Find Out Science
series)**
Kathleen Weidner Zoehfeld
(Harper Trophy)

Mountains
Seymour Simon
(Mulberry Books)

**Mountains and Our Moving Earth
(Geography for Fun series)**
Pam Robson
(Copper Beech Books)

Web Sites

Fallout
www.nationalgeographic.com/
features/98/volcanoes

Mad About Mountains
www.keswick.u-net.com/

Year of the Mountain
www.mountains2002.org/kids.html

Mountain Formation
www2.Oneonta.edu/~hessf77/
mountain.html

To find additional web sites, use a reliable search engine to find one or
more of the following keywords: **mountain, mountain climbing, Everest.**

Index